Identify Yourself!

A Six Week Reflection on Who You Are in Christ

T.M. Lotz

ISBN 978-1-105-41475-6

Identify Yourself!

Contents

INTRODUCTION

Why in the world should anyone take six weeks to study about themselves? Isn't that a rather narcissistic exercise? Shouldn't we focus more on who Jesus is than who we are?

These are valid questions.

The truth is that "who Jesus is" is someone very people-centric. The eyes of heaven are fixated on the earth. He sits at the right hand of the Father, but His conversation is about His children. It doesn't take long when hanging out with Jesus to know that His heart beats for people.

Obviously, if this is the case, and we are to imitate our Lord and Savior, we also must develop a heart for others. When we do approach these image bearers of God, the ones for whom Christ died, what shall we offer them? Listen to these words of Jesus from Luke 6:45, "A good man out of the good treasure of his heart brings forth good; and an evil man out of the evil treasure of his heart brings forth evil. For out of the abundance of the heart his mouth speaks."

We can only offer people what is in our hearts, and that will depend entirely upon who we are. If we are full of woundedness, hurt and confusion, then what comes out of us will not be very edifying to the recipients.

Insecurities drive us to manipulative and intimidating behaviors. That is why it is so important that we learn who we really are in Christ, not to pump ourselves up and make us feel good, but so that we will not inadvertently hurt others in our quest for affirmation. Then we will be safe ground that God can release His treasure into, for others can dig deeply in us without fear of triggering some unseen landmine.

Learning our identity in Christ will improve our own lives greatly. It will bring an end to internal torment, give us hope for our future and peace to sustain us along the journey. But the true beneficiaries of our quest are not ourselves, but those around us. Multitudes will discover their own destinies on the day that you "Identify Yourself!"

I AM LOVED

As the Father loved me, I also have loved you; abide in My love. If you keep My commandments you will abide in My love, just as I have kept My Father's commandments and abide in His love.

John 15:9-10

The Bible is the most romantic love story to ever be written. It is the story of God's love for mankind. The most romantic love story in existence, however, has not yet been written in full. That is the story of Jesus' trek to earth over two thousand years ago in search of an eternal relationship with you, His beloved. That story continues to unfold each day as He reaches out to you in a multitude of ways to communicate the depth and intensity of His great love.

Paul refers to this as a 'mystery.' He tells us we were given marriage as an example of how Christ loves the Church. When we join with Christ we make a commitment to be faithful and obedient to Him. He also makes a commitment. He gives us His name. We become a legal member of His family. All that He has now belongs to us. He promises from that day forth to provide for us and to protect us. Then, just like a husband to a bride, He *commits* to love us. We know that "He who has promised is faithful" (Hebrews 10:23).

Marriage is one picture of this incredible love, but God will use other earthly relationships to show us glimpses of His love as well. When we experience love from our parents, children, friends, teachers and grandparents we can accept it as a personal touch from God. The difference is that humans are faulty and unstable, whereas God's love is perfect and eternal. When people reject us, God has not rejected us.

Remember this: Every action of God towards you is motivated by love. He has never done anything to hurt you, nor will He ever do so. His love for you is without measure and without end.

WHAT DOES THE **WORD** SAY?

Read the following scriptures and write down how you feel they may apply to you and your personal walk with God.

I will betroth you to Me forever; yes, I will betroth you to Me in righteousness and justice, in loving-kindness and mercy; I will betroth you to Me in faithfulness, and you shall know the Lord.
Hosea 2:19-20

____

____

____

For I am persuaded that neither life nor death, nor angels nor principalities, nor things present nor things to come, nor height nor depth, nor any other created thing, shall be able to separate us from the love of God which is in Christ Jesus our Lord.
Romans 8:38-39

____

____

____

WHERE IS IT?

Using a concordance or Bible helps program, find one more scripture regarding today's topic which reveals your true identity.

My Personal Identification passage is: ____________________

____

I AM A CHILD OF GOD

Behold what manner of love the Father has bestowed on us, that we should be called children of God!

1 John 3:1

As Christians we have a unique relationship with the Father in that we are not only created *by* Him, but also born *of* Him. When we were born again our spirits came to life for the first time. Before that, our spirits were dead because of the sin nature which we were born into. Now we are alive in the flesh, but we are also alive in the spirit. We are children of God.

Children have a special place in the household. Although, like servants, we as children may have responsibilities and duties that are required of us, we are not servants. We have a place in the family. We have an inheritance that is ours. We have the right to approach the Father and ask whatever we wish. We have time alone with our Father one on One. Servants have to do their job so that they will be fed. We are fed, clothed and cared for, simply because we are children of the household. Our tasks are for our training, so that we will be well prepared for our future.

It is interesting to see how a family reacts when company comes over. Usually children are expected to behave very well both towards their parents and towards the visitors while they are there. Children may be required to sleep on the floor, give up a second helping at the dinner table or share a favorite toy. This is so that the visitors will feel welcome and the children will learn how to treat others. But the visitor is not part of the family, and they would never get away with taking *anything* from the children. The children are indeed the most prized possessions of the household, trained and disciplined, but guarded at all costs.

It is often the same with the household of faith. We are occasionally expected to give up our rights in order to show others our Father's goodwill, but we are the honored children, loved and cherished above all else. No one could ever take our place.

WHAT DOES THE **WORD** SAY?

Read the following scriptures and write down how you feel they may apply to you and your personal walk with God.

My son, do not despise the chastening of the Lord, nor be discouraged when you are rebuked by him; for whom the Lord loves He chastens, and scourges every son whom He receives.

Hebrews 12:5b-6

____

____

____

For you did not receive the spirit of bondage again to fear, but you received the Spirit of adoption by whom we cry out, "Abba Father."

Romans 8:15

____

____

____

WHERE IS IT?

Using a concordance or Bible helps program, find one more scripture regarding today's topic which reveals your true identity.

My Personal Identification passage is: ____________________

I AM CHOSEN

You did not choose Me, but I chose you and appointed you to go and bear fruit, and that your fruit should remain, that whatever you ask the Father in My name He may give you.

John 15:16

God has a history of 'playing favorites.' Of course, being God, He has the ability to look at the heart of man and see their true nature. So His assessment is always accurate. In the Old Testament, God chose Abraham and the nation that would come from His seed to carry His promise. He chose David to establish the kingly lineage. He chose Solomon to build His temple. In the New Testament, Jesus handpicked twelve men to be with Him as His apostles. Jesus appointed Peter to take the gospel to the nation of Israel and Paul to take it to the Gentiles. Now, God has chosen you to be His child and heir, and to carry the message of His kingdom to *your* world.

Shortly after we were married my husband and I decided to spend Christmas differently one year. We got together with those friends that were closest to us and celebrated Christmas day with them in our home. It was enjoyable to spend the day with people we had chosen to be with, not out of duty or obligation, but simply out of our desire to be together.

You are chosen. In John seventeen, Jesus prays to the Father about His desire for those whom the Father had given Him to be with him where He was going. Jesus certainly loves you, has made covenant with you and is faithful to keep His promises towards you, but beyond all that, Jesus *likes* you and <u>wants</u> to be with you! It is exciting to know that we are His family, not by chance or obligation, but by the choice of a Father who created us just as we are for His own pleasure. He still looks at what He has made and says, "It *is* good!"

WHAT DOES THE **WORD** SAY?

Read the following scriptures and write down how you feel they may apply to you and your personal walk with God.

Just as He chose us in Him before the foundation of the world, that we should be holy and without blame before Him in love, having predestined us to adoption as sons by Jesus Christ to Himself, according to the good pleasure of His will.
Ephesians 1:4-5

___

___

___

But we are bound to give thanks to God always for you, brethren beloved by the Lord, because God from the beginning chose you for salvation by sanctification by the Spirit and belief in the truth.
2 Thessalonians 2:13

___

___

___

WHERE IS IT?

Using a concordance or Bible helps program, find one more scripture regarding today's topic which reveals your true identity.

My Personal Identification passage is: ___

___

I AM SAVED BY FAITH THROUGH GRACE

For by grace you have been saved through faith, and that not of yourselves; it is the gift of God - not by works so that no one can boast.

Ephesians 2:8-9

We are saved *by* grace and *through* faith. We cannot save ourselves. There is nothing that we can do to be good enough that we would be free from sin. Jesus had to do that part for us. That is His grace.

This grace has been given to all men. Not everyone has been saved, however, because not everyone has believed the message that we are sinners and must accept Jesus' sacrifice to be set free. Only those who believe God can have this salvation. That is faith.

Romans 5:2 explains that the way we access the grace of God is through faith. God has made grace available to us – that is His part. We must accept His grace through faith – that is our part. It is a kingdom principle that applies to all things. Jesus gave us this principle while He was teaching the disciples. He said it this way: "And whatever things you ask for in prayer, believing, you will receive" (Matthew 21:22). Believing is the exercising of your faith. Receiving is the distribution of grace.

When we come to God He makes one fundamental requirement of us, that we believe His word. If we believe what He says about sin and its effects, we will obey His command to avoid it. If we believe what He says about who we are, we will act like who He says we are. Hebrews 11:6 tells us that it is impossible to please God without faith. You wouldn't be very happy with someone who accused you of lying every time that you spoke. That is what we do in our hearts when we refuse to take God at His word. Here are some points to remember about the relationship between faith and grace.

- Grace is given, not earned or bought.
- Faith is the doorway to get to grace.
- To have faith means to believe and not doubt.
- Grace has been given freely to all men.

WHAT DOES THE **WORD** SAY?

Read the following scriptures and write down how you feel they may apply to you and your personal walk with God.

Therefore it is of faith that it might be according to grace, so that the promise might be sure to all the seed, not only to those who are of the law, but also to those who are of the faith of Abraham, who is the Father of us all.

Romans 4:16

____

____

____

Therefore I say to you, whatever things you ask for when you pray, believe that you receive them and you will have them.

Mark 11:24

____

____

____

WHERE IS IT?

Using a concordance or Bible helps program, find one more scripture regarding today's topic which reveals your true identity.

My Personal Identification passage is: ____________________

I AM A NEW CREATION IN CHRIST

And He died for all, that those who live should live no longer for themselves. But for Him who died for them and rose again. Therefore, if anyone is in Christ, he is a new creation; old things have passed away; behold all things have become new.

2 Corinthians 5:15, 17

"Elderly Couple Gives Birth to Firstborn!"

"Ex-Prostitute Converts to Judaism!"

"Shepherd Boy Wins the War!"

"Christianity's Chief Prosecutor Gets Saved!"

The Bible is full of dramatic headlines when it comes to people being changed. That's because when God takes over someone's life He delights in making a big difference that is obvious to everyone. But this is no cosmetic makeover. God changes people from the inside out. That's why it sometimes takes a while to see a difference, but when it begins to show, you know it's for real.

Every one of us has a 'before' and 'after' photo

hanging up in heaven. The latter picture may not be complete yet, because the Master Artist is still working on it. The very nature of our inner being has changed. Once we were dead, now we are alive. Once we were unrighteous, now we are righteous. Once we walked in darkness, now we walk in light. All of these changes are internal. Here are some steps to let your inner beauty come out!

- **Look in the mirror every day!** James 1:23-25 tells us that when we read God's Word we get an accurate picture of who we are and what we look like. When we actually do what God's Word tells us to do, it means we remember who we truly are.
- **Dress for the occasion.** We are told to "clothe" ourselves with compassion, kindness, humility, gentleness, patience and love (Colossians 3:12, 14). It's not enough simply to have these traits deep inside of us. People need to see them *on* us.
- **Smell good!** 2 Corinthians 2:14 tells us that it is our job to spread the fragrance of the knowledge of Christ everywhere we go.

WHAT DOES THE **WORD** SAY?

Read the following scriptures and write down how you feel they may apply to you and your personal walk with God.

And the world is passing away, and the lust of it; but he who does the will of God abides forever.
1 John 2:17

____

____

____

But whoever drinks of the water that I shall give him will never thirst. But the water that I shall give him will become in him a fountain of water springing up into everlasting life.
John 4:14

____

____

____

WHERE IS IT?

Using a concordance or Bible helps program, find one more scripture regarding today's topic which reveals your true identity.

My Personal Identification passage is: ________________

____

I AM FORGIVEN AND CLEANSED

If we confess our sins, He is faithful and just to forgive our sins and to cleanse us from all unrighteousness.

1 John 1:9

The good news of the gospel is forgiveness of sin. It is the underlying theme of the New Testament that Jesus paid the price for our evil deeds and we will never have to die for our sins. We accept the blood of Jesus as our payment in full. We are not guilty of the past once we ask Jesus to forgive us. He has promised that He would forgive us.

Have you ever had a really bad dream where you had done some unspeakable, horrible act? Did you wake up in total relief to discover that it was only a dream and you really hadn't done that thing? I have, and my next thought was once again one of horror. Suddenly I realized that although I hadn't actually done that thing, the evil that would drive anyone to do such atrocities was right there in my heart! Without the cleansing power of Jesus' blood, that is what the forgiveness of sins would be like. We would be forgiven, only to know that the evil which prompted our sin was still with us and would ultimately overtake us once again.

The death of any other man may have power to save us from immediate destruction, but the death of the One perfect and sinless heart has the power to completely redeem us from all the effects of sin. He has forgiven us and He has cleansed our spirits from the unrighteousness that once dwelled within.

We do continue to struggle with a tendency towards sin due to the flesh that we live in and the world that is constantly attempting to cause us to stumble. Now, however, it is our desire to please God. The promise of 1 John 1:9 is not a one shot deal. It continues to work for us every time that we humble ourselves, seek God's face and repent of our sin. He still forgives us and cleanses us. He has no 'cleansing record' that He refers to in order to see if you have used your quota of forgiveness. His mercies are renewed every morning. God does not consider that He is being overly patient with you. As far as He is concerned, this is your first offense. That is the power of the blood of His Son applied to your life.

WHAT DOES THE **WORD** SAY?

Read the following scriptures and write down how you feel they may apply to you and your personal walk with God.

He has delivered us from the power of darkness and conveyed us into the kingdom of the Son of His love, in whom we have redemption through His blood, the forgiveness of sins.

Colossians 1:14

____

____

____

"Come now. Let us reason together," says the Lord, "though your sins are like scarlet, they shall be as white as snow; though they are red like crimson, they shall be as wool."

Isaiah 1:18

____

____

____

WHERE IS IT?

Using a concordance or Bible helps program, find one more scripture regarding today's topic which reveals your true identity.

My Personal Identification passage is: ______________________________

____

I AM JUSTIFIED & SANCTIFIED

And such were some of you. But you were washed, but you were sanctified, but you were justified in the name of the Lord Jesus and by the Spirit of our God.

1 Corinthians 6:11

Jesus is our justification. It is because He is a just man who lived a just life that He was able through an unjust death to cause unjust people to be made just in the sight of a just God. This passage in first Corinthians describes the kinds of people who are disqualified from the Kingdom of God; people like thieves, idol worshippers and the sexually immoral. Paul tells the Corinthians that they were once these kinds of people. Notice the conclusion of Paul's argument. "BUT you were washed... sanctified... justified..." Because our sins have been forgiven and our unrighteousness has been cleansed, now we are justified and sanctified. The forgiveness of sins we have been granted leaves us justified before God. The cleansing of our unrighteous spirits sanctifies us unto God.

Paul says that once the Corinthians were

adulterers, drunkards and thieves. There was a time when we were sinners. We were known to be sinners because we sinned. We are not identified by our sin any longer. In fact, our identity does not rest on our behavior at all, whether good or bad. Now we are known as justified and sanctified. Now we are known, not by our actions, but by the actions of our Lord. Our identity rests squarely on the shoulders of the One who purchased us with His blood.

In the Old Testament the priests had to wash their bodies and their clothes in a certain way in order to sanctify themselves for their priestly duties. This washing represented being cleansed from the sin of the world and set apart for service to God. Paul says that we have now been washed. It is the cleansing power of Jesus' blood that separates us from the world and sets us apart for a purpose in God's Kingdom. We are clean, not so that we can sit on a shelf and stay clean, but so that we can be used in service. We do not wash a dish just so that we can put it away. We wash dishes so they will be ready for serving the guests. Remember that we are set apart *from* the world so that we are better prepared to *serve* the world.

WHAT DOES THE **WORD** SAY?

Read the following scriptures and write down how you feel they may apply to you and your personal walk with God.

Much more then, having now been justified by His blood, we shall be saved from wrath through Him. For if, when we were enemies we were reconciled to God through the death of His Son, much more, having been reconciled, we shall be saved by His life.

Romans 5:9-10

____

____

____

But in a great house there are... vessels... some for honor and some for dishonor. Therefore if anyone cleanses himself from the latter, he will be a vessel for honor, sanctified and useful to the Master, prepared for every good work.

2 Timothy 2:20-21

____

____

____

WHERE IS IT?

Using a concordance or Bible helps program, find one more scripture regarding today's topic which reveals your true identity.

My Personal Identification passage is: ____________________

I AM SET FREE FROM SIN

But God be thanked that though you were slaves of sin, yet you obeyed from the heart that form of doctrine to which you were delivered. And having been set free from sin, you became slaves of righteousness.

Romans 6:17-18

Did you know that you are free from the power of sin? In the Christian walk, there is no such excuse as "The devil made me do it." The devil can no longer make you do anything. You are free from his control! That is wonderful news. You may have to struggle with your own desires to do things that are unholy, but you can "Just say NO." It is amazing the kind of freedom that we enjoy as Christians.

We live in a free country. In America, we enjoy wonderful privileges practically unheard of in other parts of the world. Most of us were born in America, however, and are largely unaware of how different our lives are. Many times, we not only fail to exercise the rights that were purchased for us, but we even neglect to do our part in protecting those rights. Sometimes we are told that we do not have rights in a particular area, and if we do not do our research we can be easily deceived.

Christians also fall into these traps. We take our freedom for granted, particularly if we were very young when we got saved. We fail to fight for even our most basic rights in the Christian faith. We allow the devil to gain ground in our lives by giving into sin when we should resist it. We even become deceived into believing that we cannot resist temptation because it is easier to believe the lie than to search the scriptures and exert our authority over the world, the flesh and the devil.

But we are not victims! We have the freedom to make our own choices. We are free to do the right thing in every situation. Here are some lies to avoid. They always lead to bondage.

"I just can't help it."

"Surely God understands. He knows I'm only human."

"I always give into that. It's my downfall."

"I <u>have</u> to have... (fill in the blank)!"

WHAT DOES THE **WORD** SAY?

Read the following scriptures and write down how you feel they may apply to you and your personal walk with God.

Stand fast therefore in the liberty by which Christ has made us free, and do not be entangled again with a yoke of bondage.
Galatians 5:1

____

____

____

Jesus answered them, "Most assuredly, I say to you, whoever commits sin is a slave to sin. Therefore if the Son makes you free, you shall be free indeed."
John 8:34, 36

____

____

____

WHERE IS IT?

Using a concordance or Bible helps program, find one more scripture regarding today's topic which reveals your true identity.

My Personal Identification passage is: ____________________

____

I AM REDEEMED BY THE BLOOD

And they sang a new song, saying: "You are worthy to take the scroll, and to open its seals; for you were slain, and have redeemed us to God by your blood out of every tribe and tongue and people and nation."

Revelation 5:9

In the beginning God created Adam and Eve. He created all that they would need to sustain life and many other things simply for their enjoyment. He then gave creation to Adam for him to rule over. There was an enemy who was incredibly jealous of all this control which this new creature had been given, particularly since this enemy had committed a horrible crime that had caused him to lose all of his own power. He had a little talk with Eve. Eve talked to Adam. Adam then made the decision to disbelieve what God had clearly told him and consequently, to disobey God's command. When he did this, he sold himself and all of creation into sin.

The years went by. Every person born into the world was born into the curse that Adam had brought upon us. But God had a plan to get His precious creation back. Someone had to pay the price, not only for Adam's original sin, but for all the sin that had been accumulating since that time. The cost of sin is death.

God is life. How could God die? It was necessary for God to create a man who would be perfect, without flaw, an acceptable sacrifice for the sin of mankind. So He sent His Son to be formed in flesh. He was born without the seed of man and so escaped the sin nature that mars all of creation under this dreadful curse. He was tempted as all men are tempted and was found to be without fault. He spent His brief life training men and opening their eyes to the realities of the spiritual world. Then, when the time was right, He made His sacrifice. He laid down His own life for us so that we could be reunited with God.

See, a coupon is redeemed to the store or manufacturer that issued it. It is taken back to the original owner. The blood of Jesus redeemed us to God. He was the original Owner. He created us. Mankind sold himself into the slavery of an angry, jealous power. The effects of that transaction were devastating. But the One who created us did not want to see His people suffer. So He took the necessary steps to purchase us back to Himself. We are <u>redeemed</u>, safe in the hands of Him who made us!

WHAT DOES THE **WORD** SAY?

Read the following scriptures and write down how you feel they may apply to you and your personal walk with God.

Let the redeemed of the Lord say so, whom He has redeemed from the hands of the enemy.
Psalm 107:1

____

____

____

Christ has redeemed us from the curse of the law, having become a curse for us (for it is written, "Cursed is everyone who hangs on a tree.")
Galatians 3:13

____

____

____

WHERE IS IT?

Using a concordance or Bible helps program, find one more scripture regarding today's topic which reveals your true identity.

My Personal Identification passage is: ________________

____

I AM A JOINT HEIR WITH CHRIST

The Spirit Himself bears witness with our spirit that we are children of God and if children, then heirs - heirs of God, and joint heirs with Christ.

Romans 8:16-17

In the parable of the prodigal son, there were two sons. One took what his father had given him, wasted it and found himself completely broke and wanting for even the most basic of needs. The other son worked hard and kept busy faithfully tending to his father's business. In the end, both were wrong.

Many Christians fall into one of these two categories. Some Christians use their liberty and resources to travel far away from the Lord. The Lord allows this, but He stands longingly on the road awaiting their return. The Bible says that "when he came to himself, he said, 'How many of my father's hired servants have bread enough to spare, and I perish with hunger!'" (Luke 15:17). This young lad had to come to himself to realize that it was absolutely crazy for him to live in poverty when his father was wealthy. When his thinking became clear he came to a great revelation. He was not *worthy* to be a son, but at least he could work for his father and make his living as a servant.

When he arrived, however, he only got out the first part of his planned speech. "Father, I... am no longer worthy to be called your son" (Luke 15:21). Then his father interrupted him. That was all he needed to hear. Now his father could have the kind of relationship he had been longing for. He began to make plans for a festive dinner and lavished his son with fine things. His son, overwhelmed with his own inadequacy and his father's incredible love and forgiveness, could do nothing but marvel and enjoy the grace he was receiving.

The industrious son was furious with this turn of events! He refused to participate in his brother's homecoming. Here he had labored for years without complaint. Where was his party? How could his father give so generously to this rebellious son? The answer was simple. The father gave because he was his son, not because of his performance. Both sons had an inheritance, but one never took advantage of what was his. Perhaps he did not have because he did not ask.

It gladdens the Father's heart to give to His children. He desires to celebrate with us and see us overwhelmed by His grace and mercy. Jesus' death purchased all that we need for life and godliness. "Ask and it will be given unto you" (Matthew 7:7).

WHAT DOES THE **WORD** SAY?

Read the following scriptures and write down how you feel they may apply to you and your personal walk with God.

The eyes of your understanding being enlightened; that you may know what is the hope of His calling, what are the riches of the glory of His inheritance in the saints, and what is the exceeding greatness of His power toward us who believe, according to the working of His mighty power.

Ephesians 1:18-19

____

____

____

But when the kindness and love of God our Savior toward man appeared, not by works of righteousness which we have done, but according to His mercy He saved us,... that having been justified by His grace we should become heirs according to the hope of eternal life.

Titus 2:4-5a, 7

____

____

____

WHERE IS IT?

Using a concordance or Bible helps program, find one more scripture regarding today's topic which reveals your true identity.

My Personal Identification passage is: ____________________

I AM BLESSED WITH SPIRITUAL BLESSINGS

Blessed be the God and Father of our Lord Jesus Christ, who has blessed us with every spiritual blessing in the heavenly places in Christ.

Ephesians 1:3

What are spiritual blessings? After this verse Paul continues to expound on some of those blessings; holiness, adoption, forgiveness and redemption. Jesus' death purchased many things for us that we could never have acquired on our own. It is sometimes difficult for us to grasp the significance of those treasures. Words like 'spiritual' and 'heavenly' set our minds in an ethereal mode where things are blurry and somewhat surreal.

But spiritual blessings have very concrete effects. For example, because we are forgiven of our sins and justified before God a mother can boldly approach the throne and ask the Almighty to help her children. Because we are redeemed from the curse of the law a farmer can expect his crops to produce bountifully. Because we are set free from the bondage of sin an alcoholic has the power to walk past the bar. These supernatural blessings have natural consequences.

We live in a physical world. It is easy for us to think that physical things are sturdy and unmoving while spiritual things are always changing, floating around in some plasmatic state. Actually the truth is quite the reverse. Those things which exist in the spiritual are more solid than what we see all around us. Jesus said that if we store our treasures in heaven, they would be far safer than they would in a bank or under the mattress. He did *not*, however, say we could only access them when we get to heaven!

Remember that we have access to the things that are provided us by grace through faith. That is how we receive salvation. It is also how we receive the benefits of these spiritual blessings in our lives. We read God's Word. We obey His commands. We discover what is available to us by Christ's sacrifice. We then exercise our faith, believing what God has said, proclaiming (speaking) it and watching as it comes to pass here in the physical realm.

WHAT DOES THE **WORD** SAY?

Read the following scriptures and write down how you feel they may apply to you and your personal walk with God.

Blessed are those whose lawless deeds are forgiven, and whose sins are covered; blessed is the man to whom the Lord shall not impute sin.

Romans 4:7-8

____

____

____

So Jesus answered and said, "Assuredly, I say to you there is no one who has left houses or brothers or sisters or father or mother or wife or children or lands, for My sake and the gospel's, who shall not receive a hundredfold now in this time - houses and brothers and sister and mothers and children and lands, with persecutions - and in the age to come, eternal life.

Mark 10:29-30

____

____

____

WHERE IS IT?

Using a concordance or Bible helps program, find one more scripture regarding today's topic which reveals your true identity.

My Personal Identification passage is: ____________________

I AM BLESSED COMING & GOING

Blessed shall you be when you come in, and blessed shall you be when you go out.
Deuteronomy 28:6

Do you realize that you walk in the favor of God? You do not walk *out* of the favor of God. You do not take a step to the right when you were supposed to step left and accidentally step out of God's blessing. God is with you. His favor is with you. His face shines upon you. You are His child and He is <u>for</u> you in every way.

Here in Deuteronomy chapter 28, Moses tells the people that if they obey God He is going to bless them in every place and in every way. It doesn't matter where they may go, they will be blessed. It doesn't matter what their profession is, they will be blessed. He even tells them that these blessings will "overtake" them. You have to be pretty quick to outrun the blessings of God. When God's people are obedient to Him and honor Him as their God, He becomes adamant about making it clear to all the world that this is His beloved.

In Psalm 139 David talks about this phenomenon. He tells God, "Where can I go from Your Spirit? Or where can I flee from Your presence?... If I take the wings of the morning and dwell in the uttermost parts of the sea, even there Your hand shall lead me, and Your right hand shall hold me" (Vss. 7, 9-10). He is not saying that He is trying to escape God. David is simply amazed that there is obviously no land in which his God is not Lord. There is no place where he would not be in the center of God's sight, and under His divine protection. What comfort there is in that thought! God is your God and He is leading and guiding you in every place or circumstance that you may find yourself.

Do not think that you have hit a stroke of 'good luck' when you find yourself getting an unexpected raise, being protected in the midst of danger or having unusual favor with people. These are only demonstrations of God's blessing. His principles are at work in your life, causing you to shine like the stars so that you can point others to God.

WHAT DOES THE **WORD** SAY?

Read the following scriptures and write down how you feel they may apply to you and your personal walk with God.

A highway shall be there, and a road, and it shall be called the Highway of Holiness. The unclean shall not pass over it, but it shall be for others. Whoever walks the road, although a fool, shall not go astray. No lion shall be there, nor shall any ravenous beast go up on it; it shall not be found there. But the redeemed shall walk there.

Isaiah 35:8-9

____

____

____

Trust in the Lord with all your heart, and lean not on your own understanding; in all your ways acknowledge Him, and He shall direct your paths.

Proverbs 3:5-6

____

____

____

WHERE IS IT?

Using a concordance or Bible helps program, find one more scripture regarding today's topic which reveals your true identity.

My Personal Identification passage is: ______________________

I AM ABOVE & NOT BENEATH

And the Lord will make you the head and not the tail; you shall be above only and not beneath, if you heed the commandment of the Lord your God.

Deuteronomy 28:13

In the book of Genesis, we read about the life of Joseph. As a child, he had dreams about the future, that he would be a great ruler. He told his brothers about his dreams and they began to hate him. They plotted against him and before long he found himself at the bottom of a pit. His brothers sold him into slavery. He had success with his master but his master's wife became angry with him and soon he was falsely accused and thrown into prison! He found favor with the guard and became a leader in the prison. His ability to interpret dreams eventually came to the Pharaoh's attention and he was brought out of prison and made a ruler in Egypt.

Then there's Daniel, who was taken to Babylon as a prisoner. He was put into a completely different culture but chose to take a stand for the ways of God. God continually gave him favor, even miraculously rescuing him from the fury of a power hungry king. Daniel retained a high position in the kingdom throughout the reign of three different kings. When other leaders became jealous of him and schemed to see him killed, God again delivered him. Nothing could hold him down.

Some friends of mine were once given a prophetic word that God was making them to be like Cheerios in milk. No matter how many times the enemy tried to push them under, they would simply keep popping back up to the top. This is a good picture of how God desires for us to live. We have been given buoyancy in the spiritual realm. We should always rise to the top.

I imagine that Joseph and Daniel could have sabotaged their God-given destiny if they had chosen to. What would have happened if they had gotten discouraged and said, "Why does all this bad stuff keep happening to me? God must be angry with me. I'll probably die here in prison."? When we begin to speak negatively about our circumstances, we start to act in ways that achieve the expected end. Joseph would not have served with a good attitude and prospered in prison if he had given up on God's ability to deliver him. We are called to be Cheerio Christians. Pop to the top!

WHAT DOES THE **WORD** SAY?

Read the following scriptures and write down how you feel they may apply to you and your personal walk with God.

Now He who searches the hearts knows what the mind of the Spirit is, because He makes intercession for the saints according to the will of God. And we know that all things work together for good to those who love God and are the called according to His purpose.

Romans 8:27-28

____

____

____

He shall be like a tree planted by the rivers of water, that brings forth its fruit in its season, whose leaf also shall not wither, and whatever he does shall prosper.

Psalm 1:3

____

____

____

WHERE IS IT?

Using a concordance or Bible helps program, find one more scripture regarding today's topic which reveals your true identity.

My Personal Identification passage is: ____________________

____

I AM SURROUNDED WITH FAVOR

For You, O Lord, will bless the righteous; with favor You will surround him as a shield.

Psalm 5:12

You have favor with God. A shield is used to protect something. Did you know that God is protective about you? You are not even aware of all of the attacks the enemy has launched against you because God is protecting you. For example, the enemy may try to cause strife at your workplace by instigating a misunderstanding between you and a coworker. But if God has given you favor with your boss, he may dismiss any complaint made against you. God's favor surrounds you, protecting you from harm.

God is for you! In Hebrews 12:1 after Paul has listed many of our forefathers who kept the faith despite difficult circumstances he says, "Therefore, we also, since we are surrounded by so great a cloud of witnesses, let us lay aside every weight, and the sin which so easily ensnares us, and let us run with endurance the race that is set before us." Those who have proceeded us in the faith are cheering us on as we continue on our journey.

You have a heavenly fan club! And the captain of that fan club is God Himself. No one wants to see you succeed as much as He does.

God does not sit back when you have difficulties to watch and see if you can handle it. He knows you can handle it! He has confidence in your ability to succeed. God wants *you* to see that through Him you can do all things. The favor of God towards you is so great that He will not allow any test or trial to come your way that He is not certain you are able to pass. God never sets you up to fail. He <u>always</u> sets you up to win. When God deals your hand He doesn't mind stacking the deck in your favor. He has an ace up His sleeve for you. God is in your corner. He has placed His bet and it's for you!

Whenever you find yourself in a hard spot this week start looking around for evidence of God's favor. It may be a spouse's vote of confidence, a timely phone call or a lower utility bill that frees up money for that 'surprise' expense. Whatever it is, look beyond it and see God's 'thumbs up' sign. He's waiting at the finish line.

WHAT DOES THE **WORD** SAY?

Read the following scriptures and write down how you feel they may apply to you and your personal walk with God.

When a man's ways please the Lord, He makes even his enemies to be at peace with him.

Proverbs 16:7

____

____

____

What shall we say then to all these things? If God be for us, who can be against us?... Who shall bring a charge against God's elect?

Romans 8:31, 33a

____

____

____

WHERE IS IT?

Using a concordance or Bible helps program, find one more scripture regarding today's topic which reveals your true identity.

My Personal Identification passage is: ____________________

____

I AM A DOER OF THE WORD

Therefore lay aside all filthiness and overflow of wickedness, and receive with meekness the implanted word, which is able to save your souls. But be doers of the word, and not hearers only, deceiving yourselves.

James 1:21-22

Imagine that you come home from work to find that your daughter wanted to surprise you by making a batch of chocolate chip cookies. You want to encourage her, but you can't even break the round flat disks in two with your hands, much less bite into them. "Sweetie," you ask mildly, "did you read the instructions?" "Yeah," she says, "but we didn't have any eggs and I didn't want to use the last of the milk or we wouldn't have any for cereal. So I used water instead and added some extra to make up for the eggs. Then they weren't cooking fast enough and I knew you'd be home soon so I turned up the oven."

Things come out a lot better when we follow the instructions. Often we find ourselves thinking that our way is better than God's way. Surely, if He saw the present situation He'd agree with us! So we follow our own understanding and before we know it we end up in a heap of trouble. "There is a way that seems right to a man, but its end is the way of death" (Proverbs 14:12).

The book of James tells us that when we hear the word but do not obey it we are deceived. That is because we have convinced ourselves that the way we want to go will yield better results than the way God has clearly shown us. A recipe will tell you that if you follow the directions it will yield between 2 and 2 ½ dozen cookies. The ones who write the instructions know this to be true because they have made this recipe before. We disobey God expecting that our actions will produce happiness and prosperity. The authors of the Bible make it plain to us, however, that sin inevitably yields death. They know this because they have observed it and even done it themselves.

You cannot follow the instructions if you do not read them. It is important that we regularly read God's Word because we need to be constantly reminded of His plan for our lives. Then, we must intentionally act based on the commands that we have read in the scriptures. When Daddy gets home, He'll <u>love</u> these cookies!

WHAT DOES THE **WORD** SAY?

Read the following scriptures and write down how you feel they may apply to you and your personal walk with God.

Therefore whoever hears these sayings of Mine, and does them, I will liken him to a wise man who built his house on the rock.

Matthew 7:24

____

____

____

He who has My commandments and keeps them, it is he who loves Me. And he who loves Me will be loved by My Father, and I will love him and manifest Myself to him.

John 14:21

____

____

____

WHERE IS IT?

Using a concordance or Bible helps program, find one more scripture regarding today's topic which reveals your true identity.

My Personal Identification passage is: ________________

____

I CAN DO ALL THINGS THROUGH CHRIST

I can do all things through Christ who strengthens me.
Philippians 4:13

Sometime we become intimidated when the mountains we face loom large before us. It seems that some things are much harder to deal with than others. We forget that we have been given a guarantee of victory. Regardless of what the outcome of this particular battle is, we know that we ultimately win the war.

It can help build our faith if we look back to previous battles that the Lord has granted us victory in. David used this tactic when he went out to face a much greater force than himself. He knew that he had faced enemies stronger than himself before and had won. God had given him the ability to fight the lion and the bear and to overcome them. David had confidence to fight the giant because he knew that the outcome of the battle did not rest on his power, but on the righteousness of his cause. This Philistine had to be defeated, because he was defying the Lord God of Israel. I don't think David figured it mattered very much *who* fought the Philistine. Whoever it was, they were surely destined to win because he was clearly in the wrong.

The enemies that David had to fight later in life were even more dangerous. He had to battle pride and deceit. These are the kinds of enemies that will kill a man's soul and leave his body alive to suffer. David had to fight the demonic plot carried out by well meaning allies to trick him into trying to fulfill God's plan in an ungodly way. But David continued to draw upon the righteousness of his cause so that he would not be led astray by the lure of power. David learned that he could do all things through his God. He could fight fierce competitors or he could turn the other cheek and walk away. He could live in the king's palace or he could praise God around a campfire in the wilderness. He could lead a bunch of sheep or he could lead an army of malcontents. Like Paul, he learned to be content in whatever circumstance he was in and to overcome whatever enemies he currently faced. We too, can do all things and do them to God's glory when we draw on His strength.

WHAT DOES THE **WORD** SAY?

Read the following scriptures and write down how you feel they may apply to you and your personal walk with God.

For this day is holy to our Lord. Do not sorrow, for the joy of the Lord is your strength.
Nehemiah 8:10b

___

___

___

You therefore, my son, be strong in the grace that is in Christ Jesus. You therefore, must endure hardship as a good soldier of Jesus Christ.
2 Timothy 2:1, 3

___

___

___

WHERE IS IT?

Using a concordance or Bible helps program, find one more scripture regarding today's topic which reveals your true identity.

My Personal Identification passage is: ____________________

___

I AM HAVING ALL MY NEEDS SUPPLIED

And my God shall supply all your needs according to His riches in glory by Christ Jesus.

Philippians 4:19

In Matthew chapter six Jesus tells the multitudes that God is completely aware of our need for food, drink and clothing. These were the basic needs at that time. They understood this to mean that God knew what they needed and would provide just as He does for the rest of His creation. Jesus said that our job was to seek God's kingdom and that these things would follow.

Sometimes we seem to think that God has not been updated as to the needs of mankind in our day and age. For example, if you are going to legally drive to church there are certain things that you have to have. Obviously you need a car. You also need insurance. If you have young children you are going to need an adequate car seat. These are necessary items because God makes it clear that we are to obey the authorities of our land and the authorities require these things.

Jesus' point was not that God would give you the

barest necessities for survival and nothing else, as this passage has occasionally been interpreted to mean. His point was that God is completely aware of all that you need and He is more than willing to provide those things. However, our focus should not be on acquiring the things but on acquiring God. Later, in Matthew seven, Jesus uses the analogy of a human father with his son. Not many fathers would purposely give their children something useless of even harmful when they had asked for something good. Jesus said that our heavenly Father is quite willing to give good things to those who ask Him.

We can rest assured that God desires to give us those things that we have need of. If we present our requests to Him, trust Him to provide and continue in the work He has given us to do then we will see our needs met and the Kingdom advanced at the same time. As Proverbs 10:22 states "The blessing of the Lord makes one rich, and He adds no sorrow with it."

WHAT DOES THE **WORD** SAY?

Read the following scriptures and write down how you feel they may apply to you and your personal walk with God.

"Therefore do not worry, saying, 'What shall we eat?' or 'What shall we drink?' or 'What shall we wear?' for after all these things the gentiles seek. For your heavenly Father knows that you need all these things."

Matthew 6:31-32

____

____

____

You visit the earth and water it, You greatly enrich it; The river of God is full of water; You provide for their grain, for so You have prepared it.

Psalm 65:9

____

____

____

WHERE IS IT?

Using a concordance or Bible helps program, find one more scripture regarding today's topic which reveals your true identity.

My Personal Identification passage is: ____________________

____

I AM SEEING MY WORK PROSPER

The Lord will open to you His good treasure, the heavens, to give the rain to your land in its season, and to bless all the work of your hand. You shall lend to many nations, but you shall not borrow.

Deuteronomy 28:12

It is one of the trademarks of God's hand on a person's life that they begin to prosper. Throughout the Bible there are stories of people who prospered due to their relationship with God. Abraham's possessions grew so numerous that he had to part ways with his nephew, who was also blessed with much wealth, so that their herdsmen would not argue over grazing territory. Laban's flocks prospered so much under Jacob's care that Laban did not want him to leave. Joseph's job provided him with wealth and position in the midst of a great famine, so that he was even able to provide for his extended family.

God has placed within each person talents and giftings that are unique to them. He uses these talents to provide for His people personally and also to provide for the work of God in the earth. We can have faith that the work of our hands is holy and acceptable to God and that He will bless it. God has treasures that are yet to be uncovered in every field. Scientifically, there are discoveries that God wishes to reveal to His people that would benefit mankind tremendously. George Washington Carver sought God and God opened up to him a world of wealth existing inside the humble peanut. There are many such areas that we know nothing about that the Lord will show us if we ask Him to guide us in our work. See, when God's people allow Him to prosper them in their work, *everyone* will be blessed as a result.

Prosperity is usually measured in financial gain and it is certain that God does wish to advance us in this way. However, our work prospers us in many other ways as well. We are prospered in personal development and relational skills as we work with other people who are different than us. We prosper in friendships that are built. We prosper by earning a good reputation in our communities due to our hard work. All of these are things that God can use to help spread the gospel if we have been diligent in the work He has given us to do. Our labor will be fruitful if we continue to abide in the Vine!

WHAT DOES THE **WORD** SAY?

Read the following scriptures and write down how you feel they may apply to you and your personal walk with God.

Do you see a man who excels in his work? He will stand before kings; He will not stand before unknown men.

Proverbs 22:29

____

____

____

And whatever you do, do it heartily, as to the Lord and not to men, knowing that from the Lord you will receive the reward of the inheritance; for you serve the Lord Christ.

Colossians 3:23-24

____

____

____

WHERE IS IT?

Using a concordance or Bible helps program, find one more scripture regarding today's topic which reveals your true identity.

My Personal Identification passage is: ________________

____

I AM BLESSED TO BLESS OTHERS

I will make you a great nation; I will bless you and make your name great; and you shall be a blessing. I will bless those who bless you, and I will curse him who curses you; and in you all the families of the earth shall be blessed.

Genesis 12:2-3

Throughout history God has chosen a people to carry His promise to the earth. He chose Abraham, and through Abraham He brought forth the nation of Israel. As Christians, we have been grafted into the vine through His grace. Now we too carry His great promise. But the purpose of the chosen people is not only to display the promise of God and to bask in its glory, but to distribute it liberally amongst the nations. This promise that God gave to Abraham and his descendents was that all of the families of the earth would be blessed through them.

Our world should be a better place because we are in it! It's a little known fact that you really <u>are</u> God's gift to mankind. We have been reading about the many different blessings that God has given us. These blessings are for us to enjoy, but they are also for the world to enjoy. *Through you* God has chosen to bring healing to others. *Through you* God has chosen to send forth His Word. *Through you* God has chosen to feed the hungry. *Through you* God has chosen to set free the captives who are in bondage to the devil's lies.

This is why it is absolutely vital that we discover who we are in Christ and begin to live out that reality. This is why we must discover what is ours in Christ and use our faith to access it. It is very important because God is patiently waiting to shower His love on the world through us, but we haven't tapped into His blessings fully enough for Him to do that yet.

We would love for God to use us, of course. The problem is that we just barely have enough money to cover our own expenses and maybe squeeze out our tithe. We would love to bring deliverance to those we care for, but we are still struggling to overcome unforgiveness in our own hearts. God has more than enough of all that we need stored up for us. As we learn to take Him at His Word and see His blessings start to pour out into our lives, let's remember to pass it on!

WHAT DOES THE **WORD** SAY?

Read the following scriptures and write down how you feel they may apply to you and your personal walk with God.

And God is able to make all grace abound to you, so that in all things at all times, having all that you need, you will abound in every good work.
2 Corinthians 9:8

____

____

____

But do not forget to do good and to share, for with such sacrifices God is well pleased.
Hebrews 13:16

____

____

____

WHERE IS IT?

Using a concordance or Bible helps program, find one more scripture regarding today's topic which reveals your true identity.

My Personal Identification passage is: ____________________

____

I AM THANKFUL

In everything give thanks; for this is the will of God in Christ Jesus for you.
1 Thessalonians 5:18

It is always helpful to know the will of God in a situation. Due to Paul's letter to the Thessalonians we now know that it is always God's will for us to be thankful. Is this just because God doesn't like to be taken for granted? Not likely. It is beneficial *to us* when we exercise thanksgiving.

A thankful heart is a humble heart. The proud take and expect more because they feel that they deserve it. The humble are thankful for everything they are given because they know they deserve nothing. God gives grace to the humble. He resists the proud (James 4:6). In Romans chapter one, verse twenty one, Paul tells us that one of the reasons the heart of mankind is darkened is because they choose not to be thankful to God. We need to retain a thankful heart so that our lives remain open to God's grace.

If you are having a difficult time and find yourself feeling less than thankful, you can quickly change that just by reading over the list of 'I am' statements that we are studying. Here are forty-two very good reasons to be thankful. Every one of these things that 'we are' in Christ is because of the sacrifice that Jesus made for us. We did not do anything to earn the grace that we have been given.

In the Bible we see thanksgiving being used as a tool in a variety of ways. We are told to be thankful in our personal petitionary prayer time (Phil 4:6). We are instructed to use thanksgiving in intercessory prayer for others (1 Tim 2:1). We are to be thankful in worship (Heb 13:15, Eph 5:18-21). We use thanksgiving as a way to enter into the Lord's presence (Ps 100:4). Thanksgiving is also an avenue for witnessing of God's goodness (Ps 79:13).

Here are some more reasons to be thankful:

- You have been grafted into the olive tree (Rom 11:17)
- Your name is written in heaven (Luke 10:20)
- Christ died for you while you were still a sinner (Romans 5:8)
- You have an Advocate with the Father (1 John 2:1)

WHAT DOES THE **WORD** SAY?

Read the following scriptures and write down how you feel they may apply to you and your personal walk with God.

And let the peace of God rule in your hearts, to which also you were called in one body; and be thankful.

Colossians 3:15

____

____

____

The Lord lifts up the humble; he casts the wicked down to the ground. Sing to the Lord with thanksgiving; sing praise on the harp to our God.

Psalm 147:6-7

____

____

____

WHERE IS IT?

Using a concordance or Bible helps program, find one more scripture regarding today's topic which reveals your true identity.

My Personal Identification passage is: ______________________

____

I AM FILLED WITH THE SPIRIT

And do not be drunk with wine, in which is dissipation; but be filled with the Spirit, speaking to one another in psalms and hymns and spiritual songs, singing and making melody in your heart to the Lord.

Ephesians 5:18-19

It is interesting that Paul made this a comparative statement. "Do not be drunk with wine... *but* be filled with the Spirit." What does wine have to do with the Holy Spirit, anyway? It seems to have made perfect sense to Paul when he wrote it, but what is the connection?

Wine loosens the tongue. Is it any coincidence that when someone wants to get a person to talk in the movies they get the person drunk? There is something about alcohol that causes people to talk. Have you ever known a quiet drunk? They won't quit talking, even if no one else is listening. Paul doesn't say to be filled with the Spirit and be quiet. He says to speak to one another, sing, give vocal praise to God. I've known some Christians that cause others to wonder about their sobriety. They are constantly singing, shouting exclamations of praise or talking to God. This may make many of us uncomfortable, but you have to admit, it *is* scriptural.

Drunk people are happy. Have you ever heard as much laughter and shouting as what goes on at a wild party? Most people get drunk in order to enjoy the mood enhancing quality of alcohol. Paul is trying to explain to us that Christians don't need alcohol to experience feelings of great joy. When we allow the Holy Spirit to fill us we see things in a much better light and the world truly is a wonderful place!

Drinking is a social activity. Most people prefer to drink with other people. They find that they are free to enjoy the company of other people more in their mood-altered state. It appears that Paul presumed that when this "filling" took place that the Ephesians would not be alone because he told them to speak to one another in these various ways. We can also enjoy the company of our brothers and sisters better when we are seeing them in the Spirit though the eyes of Jesus. We find that we are not so inhibited by our fear and pride. We are all more open to being our true selves and showing the love for others that comes naturally when we are together with our Christian family.

WHAT DOES THE **WORD** SAY?

Read the following scriptures and write down how you feel they may apply to you and your personal walk with God.

And when they had prayed the place where they were assembled together was shaken; and they were all filled with the Holy Spirit, and they spoke the word of God with boldness.

Acts 4:31

____

____

____

Do you not know that you are the temple of God and that the Spirit of God dwells in you?

1 Corinthians 3:16

____

____

____

WHERE IS IT?

Using a concordance or Bible helps program, find one more scripture regarding today's topic which reveals your true identity.

My Personal Identification passage is: ____________________

____

I AM LED BY THE SPIRIT

For as many as are led by the Spirit of God, these are the sons of God.

Romans 8:14

The Holy Spirit is the Comforter, Counselor and Helper which Jesus promised to send to us once He had departed. We know that the Holy Spirit is leading us because Jesus told His disciples that the Spirit would guide us into all Truth. This is one of the Holy Spirit's job descriptions – "to lead." We can be certain that He is diligent to do the work which He has been sent to do.

Sometimes we have a difficult time following because we find it hard to believe that anyone is actually leading. We must do two things in order to hear God speak to us through His Holy Spirit 1) Have faith that the Holy Spirit is here and is leading 2) Slow down, quiet down and take time to listen.

From chapter fourteen of the gospel of John to chapter sixteen, Jesus begins to 'pass the baton' over to the Holy Spirit. He starts talking more and more about this Helper who will be coming. Let's look at some of the ways Jesus said the Helper would lead us.

He will teach... (John 14:26): This includes insights given to you as you walk through circumstances, instruction from others, clarity on the scriptures and His internal nudging.

He will remind... (John 14:26): The Holy Spirit reminds us of the words Jesus has spoken when we need to hear it the most.

He will testify... (John 14:26): The Holy Spirit witnesses to us about Jesus so that we, in turn, can witness to others.

He will convict... (John16:8): He convicts us of sin, righteousness and judgment.

He will speak... (John 16:13): The Holy Spirit speaks only that which He hears from Jesus.

He will tell what is to come... (John 16:13): It is one of the functions of the Holy Spirit to reveal to God's people those things that are coming to pass.

He will glorify... (John 16:14): Jesus is exalted when the Holy Spirit is in control.

He will take and declare... (John 16:15): Jesus said that the Holy Spirit would declare to us those things the Father had given to Jesus.

WHAT DOES THE **WORD** SAY?

Read the following scriptures and write down how you feel they may apply to you and your personal walk with God.

There is therefore now no condemnation to those who are in Christ Jesus, who do not walk according to the flesh, but according to the Spirit.
Romans 8:1

____

____

____

I say then: Walk in the Spirit, and you shall not fulfill the lust of the flesh. For the flesh lusts against the Spirit, and the Spirit against the flesh; and these are contrary to one another, so that you do not do the things that you wish. But if you are led by the Spirit, you are not under the law.
Galatians 5:16-18

____

____

____

WHERE IS IT?

Using a concordance or Bible helps program, find one more scripture regarding today's topic which reveals your true identity.

My Personal Identification passage is: ____________________

____

I AM BEARING THE FRUIT OF THE SPIRIT

But the fruit of the Spirit is love, joy, peace, longsuffering, kindness, goodness, faithfulness, gentleness, self-control. Against such there is no law.

Galatians 5:22-23

What attributes were you born with? Do you have your father's nose, mom's red hair and Grandma Suzy's eyes? What kind of personality traits were you born with? Are you shy, funny, loyal or have a quick temper? Well, when you become a Christian you inherit a whole new set of traits. They are called the fruit of the Spirit. You don't usually change overnight, although you may find some things are different as soon as you get saved. You do have a new set of characteristics, however, that you can begin to grow into.

Part of that growing process requires that you begin to think and speak differently about yourself. You will not be likely to see the fruit of longsuffering in your life if you constantly say, "I'm just so *impatient*!" You might say instead, "I am still learning to be more patient." It may be a good idea to read aloud through the fruit of the Spirit periodically saying, "I <u>am</u> loving, joyful, peaceful..." This can help acquaint you with your new personality.

It is somewhat similar to a newborn fawn. A fawn is just barely born before he starts to try out his legs. Of course, he can't stand right away. He falls quite a bit. His mother will stay nearby, encouraging him. It isn't very long before he can walk. He will still be pretty wobbly for a few weeks, but he is developing strong muscles capable of leaping incredibly high.

It would be unnatural for the fawn to simply lie there and not try to stand or walk. After all, he's a deer. He has perfectly good legs and those legs would still be there even if he did not attempt to use them. It's the same way for Christians. It is only natural for us to demonstrate the fruit of the Spirit. That doesn't mean that it is completely effortless. We do have to work at it to some degree. But even if we choose not to adjust to our new personality, we still have it. We just aren't using it. So let us "grow in the grace and the knowledge of our Lord and Savior" (2 Peter 3:18).

WHAT DOES THE **WORD** SAY?

Read the following scriptures and write down how you feel they may apply to you and your personal walk with God.

That we should no longer be children,... but, speaking the truth in love, may grow up in all things into Him who is the head - Christ - from whom the whole body, joined and knit together by what every joint supplies, according to the effective working by which every part does its share, causes growth of the body for the edifying of itself in love.

Ephesians 4:14-16

____

____

____

By this My Father is glorified, that you bear much fruit; so that you will be My disciples. As the Father has loved Me, I also have loved you; abide in My love.

John 15:8-9

____

____

____

WHERE IS IT?

Using a concordance or Bible helps program, find one more scripture regarding today's topic which reveals your true identity.

My Personal Identification passage is: ____________________

____

I AM A PARTAKER OF HIS DIVINE NATURE

By which have been given to us exceedingly great and precious promises, that through these you may be partakers of the divine nature, having escaped the corruption that is in the world through lust.

2 Peter 1:4

What is God *really* like? Does He laugh a lot? Is He serious and stern? Is God emotional? How do we know? Jesus said that if we saw Him we had seen the Father. So we know that the picture we have of Jesus in the gospels is actually God in the flesh. But the gospels basically tell us what Jesus *did*. How do we know what He's like?

The Bible often refers to the Holy Spirit as the Spirit of God. The Holy Spirit is actually as much God as the Father is. We just read a list of attributes that the Holy Spirit possesses known as the 'fruit of the Spirit.' This is how we are to act because it is how our Father acts. God is certainly loving, joyful, peaceful, longsuffering, kind, good, faithful, gentle and self-controlled (Gal 5:22-23). We know that God Himself <u>must</u> have the fruit of the Spirit!

What else do we know about God's divine nature?

We know that He is merciful (Deut 4:31). God is so forgiving that Jonah loathed to tell the people of Nineveh to repent because he knew that God would forgive them (Jonah 4:2). God does not become angry easily (Joel 2:13). He is holy (1 Peter 1:16). It is the tendency of God to serve (Mat 20:28). God is always truthful (John 14:6). These are traits of God that we see in the scriptures and also in His dealings with us personally.

Our verse today tells us we can be 'partakers' of God's divine nature through the promises He has given us. In other words, because our Father has these strengths in His character, so can we. How do we obtain this nature? Through the promises of God. Promises such as those we are studying in this book. When we choose to believe what God has promised us and continually study our godly image in the mirror of His Word we will begin to truly reflect the glory of God.

WHAT DOES THE **WORD** SAY?

Read the following scriptures and write down how you feel they may apply to you and your personal walk with God.

Beloved, now we are children of God; and it has not yet been revealed what we shall be, but we know that when He is revealed, we shall be like Him, for we shall see Him as He is.

1 John 3:2

____

____

____

Therefore, having these promises, beloved, let us cleanse ourselves from all filthiness of the flesh and spirit, perfecting holiness in the fear of God.

2 Corinthians 7:1

____

____

____

WHERE IS IT?

Using a concordance or Bible helps program, find one more scripture regarding today's topic which reveals your true identity.

My Personal Identification passage is: ____________________

____

I AM KEPT IN PEACE

You will keep him in perfect peace, whose mind is stayed on You, because he trusts in You.

Isaiah 26:3

What comes to your mind when you think of peace? Is it an empty beach or maybe a quiet forest? Most of the time, our idea of peace involves a minimum of noise and activity in the midst of favorable circumstances. Unfortunately, God did not promise that we would always have favorable circumstances, but He did promise us peace.

Jesus told the disciples that the peace which He was giving them was not like the world's peace (John 14:27). There is something different about the peace of God. It can be found right in the middle of the fiercest battle of your life. The basis for our peace does not rest on the things that we can see, but on the things we do not see. Elisha was at peace even when the city of Dothan was surrounded by an army because he knew that the army of God who protected them was much larger. We can be at peace regardless of the attack the devil may send against us because the One who resides within us is far greater than the ruler of this world.

The world's concept of peace is to eliminate the battle. The world attempts to do this by accepting all of the enemies of God and not picking any fights. The idea is that if we leave the enemy alone He will leave us alone. The problem with this thought process is that the enemy's goal is not to live at peace but to conquer. There is no neutral ground where we can be safe and uninvolved. In the end, the ones who thought they were the prime negotiators of the peace treaty find themselves in bondage and slavery.

Reasons Why We Can Have Peace

1) Jesus has already conquered death, hell and the grave. (1 Cor 15:55-57; Rev 1:18)
2) God knows what we have need of before we even ask Him for it. (Mat 6:8)
3) The "accuser of the brethren" now stands condemned. (Rev 12:10)
4) When we are weak God's strength is revealed. (2 Cor 12:9; Heb 11:32-34)

WHAT DOES THE **WORD** SAY?

Read the following scriptures and write down how you feel they may apply to you and your personal walk with God.

Be anxious for nothing, but in everything by prayer and supplication, with thanksgiving, let your requests be made known to God; and the peace of God, which surpasses all understanding, will guard your hearts and minds through Christ Jesus.

Philippians 4:6-7

____

____

____

And the God of peace will crush Satan under your feet shortly. The grace of our Lord Jesus Christ be with you. Amen.

Romans 16:20

____

____

____

WHERE IS IT?

Using a concordance or Bible helps program, find one more scripture regarding today's topic which reveals your true identity.

My Personal Identification passage is: ____________________

____

I AM FORGIVING OTHERS

Let all bitterness, wrath, anger, clamor and evil speaking be put away from you with all malice and be kind to one another, tenderhearted, forgiving one another, just as God in Christ forgave you.

Ephesians 4:31-32

In Matthew chapter eighteen Jesus tells the story of the servant who was forgiven a huge debt by his king. The servant later had a fellow servant thrown into prison for a small debt that had gone unpaid. The king was very angry with the servant who had done this and reinstated his debt. The servant was then thrown into prison and handed over to torturers.

One of the reasons that we often fail to forgive others is that we do not take our own sin as seriously as God does. We tend to look at our trespasses as minor and insignificant compared to what others have done to us. This parable gives us heaven's view of our sin in comparison to the sins done against us. Obviously the debt of our sin was more than we could ever hope to pay for. This is why Jesus was sent to offer the high price of

His own life for our debts. The debt which Jesus paid for was not simply one or two sinful acts, but rather all of the sinful acts we have ever committed and, more importantly, the sinful nature inside of us which inspires those acts. All that we have ever been asked to forgive is the action of someone else who has given in, as we all have, to the sinful nature.

When the servant would not forgive, he was handed over to the torturers. Unforgiveness will inevitably do more harm to your own soul than it ever will to the one whom you refuse to forgive. Torture is a daily part of life for those who harbor unforgiveness. You know this to be true if you have ever seen someone in the store and suddenly felt sick remembering a past offense.

We do have the power to forgive because we have been forgiven ourselves. The king did not simply give the servant time to pay off his debt, as the servant had requested. He forgave his debt completely! The servant did not need the money that the other servant owed him because he was now debt free. Decide now in your heart that no one owes you anything. Learn to live debt free in the spirit!

WHAT DOES THE **WORD** SAY?

Read the following scriptures and write down how you feel they may apply to you and your personal walk with God.

Therefore, as the elect of God, holy and beloved, put on tender mercies, kindness, humility, meekness, longsuffering; bearing with one another and forgiving one another, if anyone has a complaint against another; even as Christ forgave you, so you must also do.

Colossians 3:12-13

____

____

____

And whenever you stand praying, if you have anything against anyone, forgive him, that your Father in heaven may forgive you your trespasses. But if you do not forgive, neither will your Father in heaven forgive you your trespasses.

Mark 11:25-26

____

____

____

WHERE IS IT?

Using a concordance or Bible helps program, find one more scripture regarding today's topic which reveals your true identity.

My Personal Identification passage is: ____________________

I AM WALKING IN LOVE

And walk in love, as Christ also has loved us and given Himself for us, an offering and a sacrifice to God for a sweet smelling aroma.

Ephesians 5:2

You can study the scriptures and memorize verses. You can make positive confessions about your well being and success. You can give money to every church and Christian organization that you know, but if you do not do what you do motivated by this one basic principle it will be inconsequential. Love is the foundation of the Christian walk.

It was love that prompted God to formulate an elaborate plan to rescue His rebellious creation. It was love that drove Abraham to wander, not in search of a plot of land but in search of a place close to his God. It was love that kept David in the center of God's will while on a rather confusing path to destiny. It was love that drew the prophets near to God and motivated them to record their interpretation of His heartbeat. It was love that sent Jesus to walk among us, die for us and rise again to live with us forevermore. It was love that sustained thousands since then as they gave their very lives for His Name.

We know that God is love (1 John 4:8). Jesus told the Jews that all of the Old Testament was based on the 'Love Commandments' (Mat 22:40). Those are the commandments that we are to love God with all that is in us and love our neighbor as we love our own selves. When we feel that God's actions toward mankind is not loving, it is because our understanding of love has been flawed.

As Christians, love is the basis for all that we are and all that we do. As we learn to walk in love many of the issues that we struggle with regularly will be taken care of. We will understand the nature of true love and how we can love others better as we focus on Jesus through His Word and through spending time with Him in prayer and worship.

Look for opportunities today to exercise your 'love walk.' There may be someone you see as you go about your busy day who really needs for you to slow down and take time to encourage them. You may not encounter anyone today but feel led of the Lord to pray for somebody. Walking in love usually involves sacrifice, so be prepared to give of yourself. Remember that He gave Himself for you.

WHAT DOES THE **WORD** SAY?

Read the following scriptures and write down how you feel they may apply to you and your personal walk with God.

Beloved, let us love one another, for love is of God; and everyone who loves is born of God and knows God.

1 John 4:7

____

____

____

Owe no one anything except to love one another, for he who loves another has fulfilled the law. Love does no harm to a neighbor; therefore love is the fulfillment of the law.

Romans 13:8,10

____

____

____

WHERE IS IT?

Using a concordance or Bible helps program, find one more scripture regarding today's topic which reveals your true identity.

My Personal Identification passage is: ____________________

____

I AM CRUCIFIED WITH CHRIST

I have been crucified with Christ; it is no longer I who live, but Christ lives in me; and the life which I now live in the flesh I live by faith in the Son of God, who loved me and gave Himself for me.

Galatians 2:20

When we come to the Lord, we do not only take on all of His great attributes, but we give Him all of our life and the sinful nature that goes along with it. Baptism is a beautiful picture of our own death, burial and resurrection into the new life in Christ. Because this is so, it is particularly abnormal for us to walk around in the flesh of our now dead bodies. We have been crucified with Christ and we are resurrected into a glorious new body which we live in through faith in Christ. Death is the gateway to the Christian life.

You have probably experienced this at least to some degree since you've become a Christian. There are things which were once a normal part of my life that I am completely dead to now, and for me to do those things now would feel strange. I also know that I still have some residue I have carried over from my past life that I have yet to see buried. These things hinder us from living a victorious life and from showing others what a Christian should look like.

It is necessary that we 'reckon ourselves dead' continuously in order to gain the victory that is ours in Christ. That means that although I may find myself living the same type of life that I once lived in the flesh, I simply need to remind myself that I am dead and Christ now lives in me, and try again. It is an ongoing process of dying to ourselves. This process brings us freedom, however, and we will start to see the life of Christ in us more and more.

Remember the fruit of the Spirit. Think about the attributes of the divine nature. Consider the other qualities we have been studying; love, forgiveness, peace, thankfulness. When you see these traits you know that you are living the crucified lifestyle. When you see the opposite traits manifesting in your life you know that these are areas where you still need to crucify the flesh. You can do that by repenting to God and the offended party and verbally reminding yourself of your true nature.

WHAT DOES THE **WORD** SAY?

Read the following scriptures and write down how you feel they may apply to you and your personal walk with God.

Or do you not know that as many of us as were baptized into Christ Jesus were baptized into His death? Therefore we were buried with Him through baptism into death, that just as Christ was raised from the dead by the glory of the Father, even so we also should walk in the newness of life.

Romans 6:3-4

____

____

____

For you died and your life is hidden with Christ in God. When Christ who is your life appears, then you also will appear with Him in glory.

Colossians 3:3-4

____

____

____

WHERE IS IT?

Using a concordance or Bible helps program, find one more scripture regarding today's topic which reveals your true identity.

My Personal Identification passage is: ______________

I AM A SERVANT

Yet it shall not be so among you; but whoever desires to become great among you shall be your servant. And whoever of you desires to be first shall be slave of all. For even the Son of Man did not come to be served but to serve, and to give His life a ransom for many.

Mark 10:43-45

Servanthood is not just something that Jesus did one time in history when He came to earth. It is the nature of God to serve. God spent six days before He ever made mankind creating an elaborate setting for him to live in. He made man and then decided it was not right for him to be alone. So He made a suitable helpmate for him. When Adam and Eve made their devastating decision to disobey God, God Himself fashioned a covering for them to wear. In one of the most heartbreaking books of the Old Testament, Hosea, God is shown as a rejected lover providing for His wayward bride even as she is playing the harlot.

During Jesus' life on earth He spent three years healing the sick, teaching the people and even feeding the multitudes. He raised the dead back to life. He washed

His disciples' feet. He prayed for them and also for us. Jesus is still serving us. He said that He was going to prepare a place for His people to be with Him and He is always interceding for us before the Father.

I believe that in the Trinity we see perfect servanthood. Jesus obeyed the Father's will that He come and ransom His people. The Father told Jesus to sit as His right hand until the Father should make Jesus' enemies His footstool. The Holy Spirit led and guided Jesus as He completed His journey on earth. Now the Spirit is taking those things which the Father had given to Jesus and giving them to the Church.

If our Lord and Creator spends His time serving us, then surely we should spend our time serving others. Jesus said that if we wanted to be 'someone' in the Kingdom we would have to be a servant. That doesn't mean that we start as a servant until we are promoted to a *real* position. We will always be servants. That is the way we gain authority in the spiritual realm. So if we wish to see our city, nation or family set free, then we have to start by serving them and establishing our jurisdiction.

WHAT DOES THE **WORD** SAY?

Read the following scriptures and write down how you feel they may apply to you and your personal walk with God.

Be kindly affectionate to one another with brotherly love, in honor giving preference to one another.
Romans 12:10

____

____

____

For you brethren, have been called to liberty; only do not use liberty as an opportunity for the flesh, but through love serve one another.
Galatians 5:13

____

____

____

WHERE IS IT?

Using a concordance or Bible helps program, find one more scripture regarding today's topic which reveals your true identity.

My Personal Identification passage is: ____________________

____

I AM AN IMITATOR OF CHRIST

Therefore be imitators of God as dear children.

Ephesians 5:1

We live in a society where individualism is highly esteemed. We are constantly being told, "Be yourself!" and "Do your own thing!" But Christians are supposed to be striving to become more like their Master. Even Paul the apostle told us to follow him as he followed Christ. The Lord made us to be unique individuals so that we could each live our lives in such a way as to interpret a different facet of God's vast personality to the world. However, there are some things that we should always keep in common. As Paul entreated us, we should be "like-minded." This means that all of us must work to be thankful, loving, forgiving, not high minded and obedient to God. These are traits that we cannot simply dismiss away as being, "just the way I am."

You can always tell who is popular in a culture by who the people within that culture imitate. I visited Mexico many years ago during a definite wane in the pop singer, Madonna's, career. You would never have guessed that she was no longer at the top of the charts from being in that culture. Her music was playing in every store and the style of clothing sold was obviously of her persuasion. When people step into the Christian culture, do they know that it's Jesus we admire most? Or do they hear us speak about Him, yet acting like our favorite TV stars? Do we even know how to dress, talk and act like Jesus?

In order to imitate anyone there are certain things you must do:

1) **You must follow them around.** You have to be with someone to know what kinds of things they do if you are going to do the same things.
2) **You must listen to what they say.** If you want to be like someone you have to be able to talk like they talk. You can only do that once you have spent time listening to what they have to say.
3) **You must think like they think.** This is more difficult. The disciples spent three years with Jesus and still never knew *what* He was thinking! Fortunately for us, we have two resources to assist us in this process of "renewing our minds." We have the Word of God and the Holy Spirit living inside of us, to remind us of His Words at the most opportune times!

WHAT DOES THE **WORD** SAY?

Read the following scriptures and write down how you feel they may apply to you and your personal walk with God.

Most assuredly, I say to you, he who believes in Me, the works that I do he will do also; and greater works than these he will do, because I go to the Father.

John 14:12

____

____

____

But as He who called you is holy, so you also be holy in all your conduct, because it is written, "Be holy, for I am holy."

1 Peter 1:15-16

____

____

____

WHERE IS IT?

Using a concordance or Bible helps program, find one more scripture regarding today's topic which reveals your true identity.

My Personal Identification passage is: ____________________

____

I AM THE RIGHTEOUSNESS OF GOD IN CHRIST

For He made Him who knew no sin to be sin for us, that we might become the righteousness of God in Him.

2 Corinthians 5:21

As Christians, we are told to live and act in such a way that is both pleasing to God and a witness to the world. This speaks about our behavior. However, it is important to realize that even when your behavior is not appropriate, you are still righteous before God. Our righteousness is our position in the heavenly realm. We are no longer condemned because of the sin we have committed. The blood of Jesus has cleaned us from our sin and paid the penalty for our crime. Because of Jesus' blood, God sees us as a righteous people.

Because of this righteous position before God we have the ability to come to Him at any time. We can be in the very presence of God. We can make requests of Him. We can worship Him freely. We do not have to fear when the enemy accuses us of our past, because it has been forgiven. We have power over evil because of His righteousness which He has given to us.

We still come to the Lord and repent when we have sinned, but we are no longer "slaves to sin" as we were before we got saved. We are now "slaves to righteousness." This means that, though we may sin, it is no longer in our nature to do so. Once we sinned continuously because we could not do anything different. It was simply our nature. Perhaps we occasionally 'did the right thing,' but that was the exception and not the rule. Now when we do the wrong thing, it is an exception. God has replaced our sinful nature with a nature that desires to please God.

Important Facts About Righteousness

- Righteousness is imparted to us "by grace through faith" in the blood of Jesus. We cannot earn it by our actions.
- Likewise, we do not lose our righteousness because of our sin or misbehavior.
- Righteousness is *not* righteous living. It is still necessary for us to reflect our righteousness in the way that we live and behave towards others.

WHAT DOES THE **WORD** SAY?

Read the following scriptures and write down how you feel they may apply to you and your personal walk with God.

For as by one man's disobedience many were made sinners, so also by one Man's obedience many will be made righteous.

Romans 5:19

____

____

____

For by grace you have been saved through faith, and that not of yourselves; it is the gift of God, not of works, lest any man should boast.

Ephesians 2:8-9

____

____

____

WHERE IS IT?

Using a concordance or Bible helps program, find one more scripture regarding today's topic which reveals your true identity.

My Personal Identification passage is: ____________________

____

I AM EXERCISING MY AUTHORITY

Behold, I give you the authority to trample on serpents and scorpions, and over all the power of the enemy, and nothing shall by any means hurt you.

Luke 10:19

We are often too intimidated by circumstances and our own self perceptions to even *attempt* to exercise our authority in Christ. Those who do try frequently find it to be a challenging task. Perhaps you have tried it before and it didn't work. What do you do when your authority seems to be ineffective?

One of the reasons that Jesus had such success in using His authority is that He only tried to do those things that He already saw the Father doing. In this way, He knew that it was God's desire to heal or deliver a person or to raise the dead. If something is not God's will, we don't have much of a chance of seeing it come to pass.

Here are some important factors in using our God given authority:

1) **Know God's Word.** This is essential for several reasons.

a. You must have **Faith** in order to have what you ask. You develop faith by hearing the Word (Mk 11:22-25; Rom 10:17).

b. You have to know what God says about a given situation. You also have to know what God says about *you*. When you know **God's Opinion** it is easier to see what He is doing.

c. You have to be able to **Obey** Jesus' commands. You can only do this if you are familiar with them. Jesus said if we obey His words then we truly love Him (John 14:23).

d. Jesus told us to **Abide** in His Word and then we would bear fruit that would last (John 15:7-8).

2) **Forgive Others** just as God has forgiven you. Unforgiveness is a hindrance to our prayers (Mk 11:25; Mat 6:14-15).

3) We can only use our authority in a spirit of **Love**. Loving one another is a command from God and one of the factors that empowers our faith (Gal 5:6; John 15:16-17).

WHAT DOES THE **WORD** SAY?

Read the following scriptures and write down how you feel they may apply to you and your personal walk with God.

And when He had called His twelve disciples to Him, He gave them power over unclean spirits, to cast them out, and to heal all kinds of sickness and all kinds of disease.

Matthew 10:1

____

____

____

And Jesus came and spoke to them saying, "All authority has been given to Me in heaven and on earth. Go therefore and make disciples of all nations, baptizing them in the name of the Father and of the Son and of the Holy Spirit.

Matthew 28:18-19

____

____

____

WHERE IS IT?

Using a concordance or Bible helps program, find one more scripture regarding today's topic which reveals your true identity.

My Personal Identification passage is: ________________

____

I AM WEARING THE ARMOR OF GOD

Finally, my brethren, be strong in the Lord and in the power of His might. Put on the whole armor of God, that you may be able to stand against the wiles of the devil.

Ephesians 6:10-11

It is important to realize that all Christians are involved in a war. The Bible makes this clear in several places. If you go to war without the proper equipment then your chances of winning diminish greatly. Paul lists here some of our weapons. We have already discussed several of these, truth, righteousness, peace, faith, salvation and God's Word. It isn't enough just to know that we have them. We must also be able to use them effectively when we are under attack.

When David went to war against Goliath he could not wear Saul's armor because he was not accustomed to it. You cannot wait until it's time to go to war to learn how to use your armor. You need to be familiar with it long before and know how to walk in it.

We can practice being truthful in our everyday lives. We want to tell ourselves the truth and not be deceived by common lies that we have heard for years. We also need to be truthful with others and take all things to God's Word to determine its validity. We must guard our hearts with the reality of our righteousness. We have a place before God that Jesus purchased for us and no one can ever take that away. Our identity is based on our standing with God, not what other people may think or say.

The good news of peace can direct our footsteps every day. Because we now have peace with God we can be at peace with ourselves and peace with others. We can also share the great message of God's salvation in quietness of soul and confidence because of this peace that is within us. We can exercise our faith in the 'little' things of life so that we will be able to use it efficiently when the enemy tries to deliver a fatal blow. We must keep the knowledge of our salvation foremost in our minds and use it as a filter to guard our thinking. The Word of God is our sword. When we speak His Word into our lives and situations we can see victory in the battle!

WHAT DOES THE **WORD** SAY?

Read the following scriptures and write down how you feel they may apply to you and your personal walk with God.

Are not five sparrows sold for two copper coins? And not one of them is forgotten before God. But the very hairs of your head are all numbered. Do not fear therefore, you are of more value than many sparrows.

Luke 12:6-7

____

____

____

For though we walk in the flesh, we do not war according to the flesh. For the weapons of our warfare are not carnal but mighty in God for pulling down strongholds.

2 Corinthians 10:3

____

____

____

WHERE IS IT?

Using a concordance or Bible helps program, find one more scripture regarding today's topic which reveals your true identity.

My Personal Identification passage is: ________________

I AM DELIVERED FROM THE ENEMY

He has delivered us from the power of darkness and conveyed us into the kingdom of the Son of His love.

Colossians 1:13

Jesus called the devil the father of lies (John 8:44). His primary weapon is still deception. The devil would love to convince you that he still has power over you despite the fact that you have been born again. But this is great news – you are delivered from the enemy! In this one statement there are many truths that will bring you freedom. Here are just a few:

You can resist sin. Sure, you still struggle with sin sometimes, but you are far from powerless! You *can* choose to do right. Anytime that you hear a voice telling you that you cannot have victory over 'this one thing' you know that it's the liar speaking.

The devil cannot harm you. Many people have fallen into a life of bondage to ritual and superstition because they did not know this fact. We have authority over the enemy. Do not fear his tactics. Jesus is the conqueror and He takes care of His own!

You can be healed. Healing is a part of the salvation that Jesus purchased for us. Sometimes it takes time and effort to acquire our healing, but do not think that you have to suffer because of the effects of sin or because the devil has some sort of power over your body. Healing <u>can</u> be yours.

Your emotions are not the devil's stomping grounds. There are many factors that influence how we feel. Circumstances, chemicals and relationships all play a part in our emotions. We do not have to be ruled by strong emotion, however. We can take the initiative and change our emotions using God's Word.

You can be sure of your salvation. This is an area where many people have let the devil trick them into selling their birthright by convincing them that they were not saved. God does not lie. If He says He will forgive sin then He truly forgives sin. All He requires is that we believe Him and take Him at His Word.

WHAT DOES THE **WORD** SAY?

Read the following scriptures and write down how you feel they may apply to you and your personal walk with God.

To perform the mercy promised to our fathers and to remember His holy covenant, the oath which He swore to our father Abraham; to grant us that we, being delivered from the hands of our enemies, might serve Him without fear.

Luke 1:72-74

____

____

____

Be sober, be vigilant; because your adversary the devil walks about like a roaring lion, seeking whom he may devour. Resist him, steadfast in the faith, knowing that the same sufferings are experienced by your brotherhood in the world.

1 Peter 5:8-9

____

____

____

WHERE IS IT?

Using a concordance or Bible helps program, find one more scripture regarding today's topic which reveals your true identity.

My Personal Identification passage is: ____________________

I AM OVERCOMING BY THE BLOOD

And they overcame him by the blood of the Lamb and the word of their testimony, and they did not love their lives to the death.

Revelation 12:11

In this book we have spent much time studying the victorious life. We have examined how to have healing, finances, even deliverance from demonic forces. But there are those who will use God's principles to obtain these things and live a good life but still miss the most important point. To overcome the world is not equivalent to overcoming poverty, sickness and oppression. To overcome the world means to hold fast to the great truth that Jesus is Lord of all creation and has redeemed us from our sin.

We want to live in freedom so we may be shining examples of God's goodness to a world in darkness. But this accomplishment is the greatest victory that we can ever have – that we allow nothing, not even the death of our earthly bodies, to silence our profession of faith.

You may never have to face the barrel of a gun and confess Jesus. In fact, for many people this test would be significantly easier than the test of confessing Him in our daily lives. What are you willing to sacrifice for your adamant stand for Christ? Will you lay down the acceptance of friends and family? What about the love of a spouse or children? Would you risk your job, as many people do in other countries when they become Christians?

When Paul said, “I die daily” in 1 Corinthians 15:31, it was this phenomenon that he was talking about. The concept of martyrdom was not a difficult one for him to accept because he had given up his life a long time ago. He knew that once they killed his body he would be present with the Lord and his struggle would be over forever. It is the daily commitment to lay down all of one’s hopes, dream and rights that produces a living martyr. But when we think of the high price that was paid for us, the precious, innocent blood of Jesus – and we consider the change He made within us – we have the power to love God even more than our own lives.

WHAT DOES THE **WORD** SAY?

Read the following scriptures and write down how you feel they may apply to you and your personal walk with God.

These things I have spoken to you, that in Me you may have peace. In the world you will have tribulation; but be of good cheer, I have overcome the world.

John 16:33

____

____

____

For whatever is born of God overcomes the world. And this is the victory that has overcome the world – our faith. Who is he that overcomes the world, but he who believes that Jesus is the Son of God?

1 John 5:4-5

____

____

____

WHERE IS IT?

Using a concordance or Bible helps program, find one more scripture regarding today's topic which reveals your true identity.

My Personal Identification passage is: ________________

____

I AM WALKING BY FAITH

While we do not look at the things which are seen, but at the things which are not seen. For the things which are seen are temporary, but the things which are not seen are eternal... For we walk by faith, not by sight.

2 Corinthians 4:18; 5:7

All that we have been given as a result of Jesus' sacrifice exists first in the unseen realm. It is only by faith that we can even access our salvation. If you do not believe in what is unseen you cannot be a Christian because all that we trust in is unseen. The Jews asked for a sign. They had several signs already but refused to believe. In Jesus' parable of Lazarus and the rich man, the rich man wanted Abraham to send Lazarus to warn his brothers. Abraham said that if they would not believe the prophets, neither would they believe one who had risen from the dead. Faith is essential to being a Christian, and it exists in the heart. External circumstances will not produce faith because they only affect the mind. The Word of God, however, can penetrate to the heart and bring about faith.

When we exercise our faith things that are seen begin to change. These things are only temporary. The unseen things which we have been given by faith; salvation, righteousness, healing, forgiveness, provision, joy, peace, etc., are eternal. They are always there and always available to us. We do not see them, but we know they are and that they are ours because of Jesus.

We plan the pathways of our lives based on this faith. If I did not have faith that God has promised to provide for me when I seek His Kingdom first then I would have pursued a degree in computer programming rather than ministry. If the missionary did not have faith in God's protection and healing he would never take his children to a disease stricken country. If we did not have faith in God's promise of salvation we would still be trying to do more good works than bad so we could earn our way into heaven. You may not feel like you've ever taken a step of faith, but if you have prayed and asked Jesus into your heart then you have indeed used your faith. Since Jesus told us it only requires a tiny amount of faith to move mountains, then you certainly have enough to walk daily trusting God's promises!

WHAT DOES THE **WORD** SAY?

Read the following scriptures and write down how you feel they may apply to you and your personal walk with God.

But without faith it is impossible to please Him, for he who comes to God must believe that He is, and that He is a rewarder of those who diligently seek Him.

Hebrews 11:6

____

____

____

Jesus said to him, "Thomas, because you have seen Me, you have believed. Blessed are those who have not seen and yet have believed."

John 20:29

____

____

____

WHERE IS IT?

Using a concordance or Bible helps program, find one more scripture regarding today's topic which reveals your true identity.

My Personal Identification passage is: ____________________

____

I AM TAKING EVERY THOUGHT CAPTIVE

Casting down arguments and every high thing that exalts itself against the knowledge of God, bringing every thought into captivity to the obedience of Christ.

2 Corinthians 10:5

Dr. Ted Estes often says that "The battlefield on which we wage our warfare is the mind." The more we learn about the intricate workings of the brain through science the more obvious this becomes. Our thoughts affect everything about us, even our health. Could this be why Paul urges us to renew our minds with the truth found in God's Word? If we allow any negative thought to freely have reign in our minds we will suffer mentally, spiritually and physically. We must have a filter on our minds, the same way many of us do on our internet systems. Certain things are permissible and certain things do not even get past the front door.

What does Paul say should not be allowed to have access into our thought lives? Anything that exalts itself against, not only God, but the knowledge of God, is unacceptable for us as Christians to think about. That means that if God says that something is a fact, but another idea comes along to suggest that it is not actually a fact, then it must be taken captive.

We have actually been learning how to do this as we study what God's Word has to say about who we are. Personal identity is one of the primary areas that the devil tries to confuse. We are learning who God says we are so that when thoughts come to our minds that are contrary to what He said we know not to entertain those thoughts. The way that we take a thought captive is to speak the truth instead.

Please be aware that the world we live in is prevalent with thoughts and ideas which are opposed to God. There are many lies in this world about who God really is and what He is like. If you do not use the Word of God as the final judge for all truth you will be easy prey for the enemy. Jesus said that His sheep would know His voice and the voice of a stranger they would not follow. The sheep know the shepherd's voice because they are familiar with it. Let's tune into God and tune out of the world!

WHAT DOES THE **WORD** SAY?

Read the following scriptures and write down how you feel they may apply to you and your personal walk with God.

For to be carnally minded is death, but to be spiritually minded is life and peace. Because the carnal mind is enmity against God; for it is not subject to the law of God, nor indeed can it be.

Romans 8:6-7

____

____

____

For the Word of God is living and powerful, and sharper than any two-edged sword, piercing even to the division of soul and spirit, and of joints and marrow, and is a discerner of the thoughts and intents of the heart.

Hebrews 4:12

____

____

____

WHERE IS IT?

Using a concordance or Bible helps program, find one more scripture regarding today's topic which reveals your true identity.

My Personal Identification passage is: ____________________

____

I AM RENEWING MY MIND

And do not be conformed to this world, but be transformed by the renewing of your mind, that you may prove what is that good and acceptable and perfect will of God.

Romans 12:2

Knowing the will of God for our lives is an issue that most of us struggle with from time to time. Sometimes it does not seem as clear as we think it should be. According to this verse, knowing God's will is easier when you have renewed your mind. How do we do that? It seems that there are three steps in this passage.

1) **Do not be conformed.** Nothing is conformed into a given shape without applying pressure. Apparently, there is an intentional force pressuring us into taking on a shape contrary to our natural tendency. It is up to us to resist the molding techniques applied by the world system. What are those techniques? Primarily, they are the spreading of ideas through television, education, politics, etc. Be aware of the world's propaganda.

2) **Be transformed.** It is much more difficult for the world to conform us to its mold when we have been

transformed. Jesus said that which is born of flesh is flesh, but what has been born of the Spirit is no longer flesh, but spirit (John 3:6). Paul told us if we walk after the Spirit we will not do the works of the flesh anymore (Gal 5:16). Flesh is very moldable. How do you mold spirit matter?

3) **Renew your mind.** We can be transformed by learning to think differently. Jesus said that the words He spoke were actually spirit (John 6:63). He also told His disciples that they were clean because the words He had spoken to them had cleansed them (John 15:3). We need to think about the Word of God more than we are thinking about natural things. As long as we spend the majority of our time thinking about natural things we will continue to walk in the flesh more than we walk in the Spirit.

This transforming process will help us to think more like God thinks, so His will becomes more obvious to us.

WHAT DOES THE **WORD** SAY?

Read the following scriptures and write down how you feel they may apply to you and your personal walk with God.

Finally, brethren, whatever things are true, whatever things are noble, whatever things are just, whatever things are pure, whatever things are lovely, whatever things are of good report, if there is any virtue and if there is anything praiseworthy – meditate on these things.

Philippians 4:8

____

____

____

I have given them Your word; and the world has hated them because they are not of the world, just as I am not of the world.

John 17:14

____

____

____

WHERE IS IT?

Using a concordance or Bible helps program, find one more scripture regarding today's topic which reveals your true identity.

My Personal Identification passage is: ____________________

I AM THE LIGHT OF THE WORLD

You are the light of the world. A city that is set on a hill cannot be hidden. Nor do they light a lamp and put it under a basket, but on a lampstand, and it gives light to all who are in the house. Let your light so shine before men, that they may see your good works and glorify your Father in heaven.

Matthew 5:14-16

We have a job while we are on the earth. Our job is to reflect the light of the Son so brightly that all of the world can see Him clearly. In order to do this we must make sure that there is nothing in our lives that would eclipse His glory. We are a city on a hill. Many Christians try to live inconspicuously so they will not have to live holy lives. But Jesus says that we will not be hidden. The world *will* see us. The question is what will they see?

What you say: God is either glorified or blasphemed by the words of our mouths. People are listening to the way we speak. They want to know what kinds of things dominate our conversation. The world knows as well as the Church that we speak out of the abundance of our hearts. They know that by listening to us they will find out what is inside of us.

What you do: People are also watching our actions to see if they line up with what we say. We might talk about forgiving others, but how do we treat *them* when they make a mistake? Do we consider the well being of other people or do we look to our own interests first. Do we actually put God first in our lives with prayer and Bible study or do we just belong to some sort of a religious club?

How you live: Everyone really wants to know what goes on behind the scenes. They can usually tell by our behavior towards our spouses and children. They also can tell more about us by watching the attitude with which we approach our jobs. People see how we spend our money and know instantly what is most important to us. They hear us talk about where we go, what we do in our spare time and what we saw on television. All of these details speak volumes to others about who we really are.

We are God's tool for getting the word out to mankind. Believe it or not, they are listening. We won't be hidden, so we might as well shine!

WHAT DOES THE **WORD** SAY?

Read the following scriptures and write down how you feel they may apply to you and your personal walk with God.

Walk in wisdom toward those who are outside, redeeming the time. Let your speech always be with grace, seasoned with salt, that you may know how you ought to answer each one.

Colossians 4:5-6

____

____

____

Do all things without complaining and disputing, that you may become blameless and harmless, children of God without fault in the midst of a crooked and perverse generation, among whom you shine as lights in the world, holding fast to the word of life, so that I may rejoice in the day of Christ that I have not run or labored in vain.

Philippians 2:14-16

____

____

____

WHERE IS IT?

Using a concordance or Bible helps program, find one more scripture regarding today's topic which reveals your true identity.

My Personal Identification passage is: ____________________

____

I AM A ROYAL PRIESTHOOD

But you are a chosen generation, a royal priesthood, a holy nation, His own special people, that you may proclaim the praises of Him who called you out of darkness and into His marvelous light.

1 Peter 2:9

God has done a marvelous thing in these last days. He has chosen not to dwell in a temple made by man but to live inside of people who have been redeemed by His Son. He has even made us to be His priests, offering up sacrifices of praise to His name. We are all holy people, set apart to God for His purpose, that we would proclaim His name throughout all the earth.

This job has not been given to the pastor or even the evangelist, but to everyone who has been saved by the blood of Jesus. All of us have a message to give to the world. We have been called out of darkness and into light. Each of us made a journey to get to the place where we are now. We have a story to tell about this journey and how our lives are different since we took that path.

We may tell our story in song. Some of us may tell

the story to the poor and the hungry as we serve a much needed meal. Someone's story may be portrayed on a canvas with strokes of a brush. A fisherman may tell his story while he is out in the boat with his buddies. A businessman may share his story with colleagues who are curious about his success.

Our offerings look different than those of the Old Testament priests, but they are precious to God. The priests of the Old Testament also interceded for the people. Remember to pray for those around you. You don't know, one of the people you pray for may not have anyone else in the world praying for them. You can be the one to seek God on their behalf and bring about positive change in their lives. It is also our job and privilege to worship God. It is like sweet incense to God when His people worship them of their own free will because they simply love and adore Him. Remember you are God's holy priest. You are always welcome in His courts.

WHAT DOES THE **WORD** SAY?

Read the following scriptures and write down how you feel they may apply to you and your personal walk with God.

Having been built on the foundation of the apostles and prophets, Jesus Christ Himself being the chief cornerstone, in whom the whole building, being fitted together, grows into a holy temple in the Lord, in whom you also are being built together for a dwelling place of God in the Spirit.

Ephesians 2:20-22

____

____

____

Jesus Christ, the faithful witness, the firstborn from the dead, and the ruler over the kings of the earth, to Him who loved us and washed us from our sins in His own blood, and has made us kings and priests to His God and Father, to Him be glory and dominion forever and ever. Amen.

Revelation 1:5-6

____

____

____

WHERE IS IT?

Using a concordance or Bible helps program, find one more scripture regarding today's topic which reveals your true identity.

My Personal Identification passage is: ____________________

I AM MORE THAN A CONQUEROR

Yet in all these things we are more than conquerors through Him who loved us.

Romans 8:37

"For better or for worse, for richer or for poorer, in sickness and in health, 'till death do us part." These are the standard vows that couples take when they get married. Now listen to the vows God makes over you based on Romans 8:35-39 and Matthew 28:20.

"In tribulation and distress, in persecution and famine, in nakedness, peril and sword, neither life nor death, angels nor principalities nor powers, things present nor things to come, height nor depth, nor any created thing shall separate you from My love. And lo, I am with you always, even until the end of the age."

We may encounter difficulties in life. Jesus even told us that we would have troubles in the world. But we also have the promise that through Him we can conquer anything that may come our way. Nothing will ever separate us from His love. It is His love that gives us strength to face any hardship and to persevere through it. Nothing can happen to us that is stronger than the power of His love.

Let's look at Romans 8:35-37 in a more modern light:

What shall separate us from the love of Christ? Shall family problems of corporate downsizing, car trouble or mental anguish, poor health or broken relationships, identity crisis, hurtful rumors, economic failure, political upheaval or destructive weather patterns? In all of these things we are more than conquerors through Him that loved us.

How do we know that we will conquer? Because God is able to cause us to have victory. As long as we are trying to follow Him He will make us victorious. We have been frightened because we knew that the devil doesn't play fair and he's stronger than us, anyway. But since Jesus has been given authority over all things, He no longer plays fair, either. He doesn't mind stepping into the ring when we are losing miserably and putting a quick end to the devil's game. He is our big brother and He is looking out for us. We can rest assured He has our back!

WHAT DOES THE **WORD** SAY?

Read the following scriptures and write down how you feel they may apply to you and your personal walk with God.

For this reason I also suffer these things; nevertheless I am not ashamed, for I know whom I have believed and am persuaded that He is able to keep what I have committed to Him until that Day.
2 Timothy 1:12

____

____

____

Now to Him who is able to keep you from stumbling, and to present you faultless before the presence of His glory with exceeding joy, to God our Savior, who alone is wise, be glory and majesty, dominion and power, both now and forever. Amen.
Jude 24-25

____

____

____

WHERE IS IT?

Using a concordance or Bible helps program, find one more scripture regarding today's topic which reveals your true identity.

My Personal Identification passage is: ______________________

____

I AM HEALED BY JESUS' STRIPES

Who Himself bore our sins in His own body on the tree, that we, having died to sins, might live for righteousness - by whose stripes you were healed.

1 Peter 2:24

Sickness and disease are a result of the fall of mankind into sin. That doesn't mean that every time you get a cold it's because you have sinned. It means that the presence of sickness in the earth is a result of the first sin. When Jesus died on the cross He delivered us from the curse of the law. We know that Jesus delivered us from condemnation, mental torment and poverty, but sometimes it is more difficult for us to believe that He also delivered us from sickness.

Jesus purchased our healing for us on the cross. 'Salvation' does not only mean we won't go to hell. That word includes healing, deliverance from demons and freedom from poverty. We already have healing. Jesus bought it for us, but we seldom use it. Wouldn't you be sad if you had bought someone a costly and much needed gift that they refused to take? We should not refuse

Jesus' gift of healing.

Like all the other gifts we have discussed that Jesus provided for us, we access our healing by faith. Do you ever wish that there was just *some* other way to obtain God's grace? Surely it would be easier to work for it somehow, maybe give a certain amount of money or walk a few thousand miles. It's really so simple. Yet believing God can be so hard!

But God requires the same thing from us in the area of healing that He does in the rest of the Christian walk. He wants us to believe Him and take Him at His Word. Healing has been given. That does not mean we cannot ask God for healing since it has been given or that you are a bad person if you do not receive your healing. But do not doubt that healing has been purchased at the cross and it can be ours! Here are some points to help build your faith for healing:

- Healing was a regular part of Jesus' ministry on earth.
- Jesus gave His disciples the ability to heal others as well.
- The disciples continued to heal after Jesus ascended.
- Healing was a common occurrence in the early church.
- James instructed that healing prayer be made for those who were sick in the church.

WHAT DOES THE **WORD** SAY?

Read the following scriptures and write down how you feel they may apply to you and your personal walk with God.

And believers were increasingly added to the Lord,... so that they brought the sick out into the streets and laid them on beds and couches, that at least the shadow of Peter passing by might fall on them. Also a multitude gathered from surrounding cities to Jerusalem, bringing sick people and those who were tormented by unclean spirits, and they were all healed. Acts 5:14-16

____

____

____

Is anyone among you sick? Let him call for the elders of the church, and let them pray over him, anointing him with oil in the name of the Lord. And the prayer of faith will save the sick, and the Lord will raise him up. And if he has committed any sins, he will be forgiven.

James 5:14-15

____

____

____

WHERE IS IT?

Using a concordance or Bible helps program, find one more scripture regarding today's topic which reveals your true identity.

My Personal Identification passage is: ____________________

www.ingramcontent.com/pod-product-compliance
Ingram Content Group UK Ltd.
Pitfield, Milton Keynes, MK11 3LW, UK
UKHW041940190726
13854UKWH00004B/1696

9 781105 414756